'from Suicide to God's Side'

Angela Goodman Foxworth

'from Suicide to God's Side'

ॐ

Angela Goodman Foxworth

'from Suicide to God's Side'

Copyright © 2016 Biblion Publishing LLC

Biblion Publishing LLC

Unless otherwise indicated, scripture quotations are from the Holy Bible, King James Version.

ISBN-978-1-940698-9-0

ACKNOWLEDGEMENTS

Without God, I would not be here. Without God I would not have survived my journey. So I must first Thank God for being God in my life and for giving me the precious gift of life, and the desire to share my story 'from Suicide to God's Side'

I give a special Thank You to my husband, Shawn Foxworth, who is my #1 supporter. You, my dear, my love, my protector, my friend are one of the reasons I am who I am today. Thank you for pushing me to keep moving forward. Thank you for being my Man of God and my greatest inspiration.

To my brother, my Pastor, the Man of God who covers me, James F. Goodman, I say Thank you. As a young girl you have been the big brother who always looked out for me; but when you became my Pastor, you also became my counselor, my intercessor, my Spiritual father, and the vessel God used to teach me His Word and His way. I am Free today because you allowed God to use you to save my life.

To my sister-in-law, my First Lady, Tonya Goodman, I say Thank you. As my sister and my friend you were there for me through it all, but as my First Lady, you were the one who prayed for me and with me. You never gave up and you never stopped saying what God said. I found strength to keep going because of you.

To my parents, Robert & Helen Goodman, whom without there would be no Angela. Loved, nurtured, and cherished by the greatest gifts God could have given anybody, I am honored to call them mama and daddy. My mother passed away before my book was completed but I dedicate this entire book to her memory. I love you mama and daddy.

To *my5starz,* my children: Tenisha, Cordell, David, Crystal, and Tiffany. You all will never know just how much I love or how proud I am of each of you. My journey was not easy, and I know that there were some very dark moments that you all went through because of me. But, please know that I appreciate the love and strength that you all showed and gave me each time I went through my lowest points. The five of you were always there, and I thank God for blessing me with 5 Beautiful Strong Dynamic Awesome STARZ.

"I thank God for this day." What now seems like a life-time ago, I couldn't say that. There was a time when everyday that I "woke up" I was angry; every waking moment I spent thinking about dying. I lived with, nursed, nurtured, and held on to so much pain, hurt, and anger that I didn't know or cared enough to know that I could LIVE the life that God promised me in His Word. Follow me on this journey and see God's love demonstrated and manifested.

Who Am I?
My name is Angela Goodman-Foxworth. I am a 51 year old woman with 5 adult children, 9 step-children, and 21 grandchildren. I have been married to my husband, Shawn Foxworth, since March 20, 2010.

In June of 1983 I graduated from high school, turned 18, and got married to my first husband; then I gave birth to my **first** child one month later. I got saved at the age of 17 and had my **fifth** child by the age of 22.

I loved God, lived for God, and did all that I knew and was taught about God's Word. However, I later learned that I had put more of myself, my confidence, my hopes, and my dreams in my then-husband, rather than in God. So when life happened, and my marriage began to fail, I became really angry with God and walked away from Him.

During that time...is when I began believing the voice of the enemy that I was worthless and everyone, especially my children, would be better off if I were dead.

It was the summer of 1995, I remember it well because it was the **FIRST** time I attempted suicide. Yes I was a mother of five young children, a daughter of two wonderful parents, and a wife to a man I thought hated me. I didn't believe nor did I care that God loved me. I was convinced that my children would have been better off if I were dead. So I overdosed on pills in my office after-hours, hoping that by the time anyone found me the next day I would be gone. But two co-workers who were not supposed to be at work found me that evening and rescued me (against my will).

I didn't know it then but waking up in the hospital getting my stomach pumped would become a common and regular occurrence for me.

Oh yeah, did I say that was the First time?

In August of 1995 I was raped at knife-point, lost my best friend, Munchie, after an aneurism burst in her head, and my marriage was in turmoil. I was indeed a failure and had deserved everything that was happening to me. The enemy had even convinced me that my best friend died to get away from me and I believed him. I had begun carrying a blade, cursing like a sailor, and was as mean as a rattlesnake. During this time of my life I hated myself and everyone around me. I was a walking time-bomb destroying everything and everyone in my path.

As I sit here thinking (not looking) but THINKING back from where God brought me, I realize that if the enemy had his way, I would not to be here. But as I sit here looking at all of my prayers on my wall, some written as far back as 1998, I can't help but be reminded of the turmoil, tribulations, troubled mind, failed tests, defeated mindset, and pain that I once called ME.

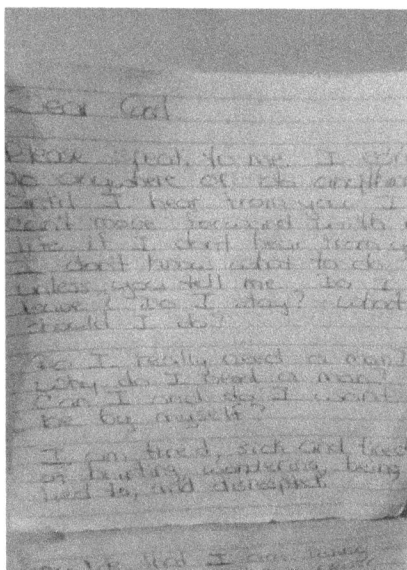

I can't help but to believe now that even during my lowest moments I was still writing prayers to God as if a part of me had recognized that He would help me.

In 1995, my mind and my life were so filled with hurt and self-hatred that I attempted suicide at least 15 times. I know, you are probably saying if I really wanted to die I could have done so successfully at any given time with a knife or gun. Yeah you're right. But I will admit that I WAS a person who was afraid of pain and blood (no I was not a "woman about mine"). I wanted to lie down and transition right out of this world and into eternity. So I tried and tried and tried and tried and tried over and over again to end my life by overdosing on pills. Besides, I didn't want my suicide to appear obvious because I wanted my children to be able to collect on the life insurance policy.

From 1995 – 1998 my life spun totally out of my control. I had begun drinking alcohol, partying in clubs, and doing anything and everything that I thought I was big and bad enough to do. If the truth be told, I didn't care who I hurt while I was doing me. I was miserable and I wanted to bring down as many people as possible.

In 1998, when I was at one of my lowest points, I had attempted to commit suicide more times than I can even remember. However, each time I tried, God sent someone to find me. So I became very angry with God and began to ask Him, "WHY? Why won't You let me die?"

Guess what His answer to me was?

It's 1998, I'm now divorced after 15 years of marriage, 5 young children, making $9.00 an hour, feeling defeated and existing in a life that I can't wait to end. Here I am mad with God because HE failed me. After all, *His Word says He'll never leave nor forsake me, right?* Heard it my whole life. But guess what? <u>I WAS ALONE.</u> Did He leave me? Did He forsake me? Was I a victim? Or was I living out the consequences of decisions that I MADE FOR MYSELF? ALL I knew at that time was you may keep saving me now, but I WILL DIE, it's only of matter of when. (I even said to God once, "I'll keep trying until You get tired of saving me.")

After so many failed suicidal attempts I asked God, "Why won't You let me die?" The answer came one Saturday morning around 8:00am. I went to the empty home my ex-husband and I had together and had taken an overdose of pills (prescription and over-the-counter combined) the night before, laid down, and waited to die. Well I didn't die, I ONLY fell asleep. I was awaken that morning by the ringing of my phone. On the other end was my brother, Porkey Goodman. He asked me where was I and when I wouldn't tell him he said I know you tried to hurt yourself last night but God is not going to let you die *because He has something for you to do.*

Filled with so much anger and disappointment I hung up the phone crying and said, "God I don't want to live but You won't let me die. Please tell me what good am I to You or to this world? But not knowing how to HEAR God, I continued on the destructive path I was on for the next 10+ years.

I continued to allow the enemy to convince me that I was not worth living or that no one loved me, and I even hated myself. But I must admit that through all of this, my children nor my family would give up or walk away from me.

So after my divorce from my first marriage I moved myself and my daughters to Washington DC to try to "start my life over". I called my ex-husband and asked him to please allow my sons to move in with him because I could not teach them how to be men. (The real truth was I was afraid to move them to DC with me for fear of losing them to the streets). At that time I had never lived anywhere but Sumter SC and I really didn't know what to expect in a new place.

I had convinced myself that if I leave Sumter, I would stop trying to commit suicide and would live a happier life. WRONG!!! I didn't realize then that I was taking *me* with me to DC and the mindset that I had stayed with me everywhere I went.

The enemy didn't care that I had located to a new region, he continued to talk to me and I continued to listen to him. He was my buddy, my pal, my friend, my enemy, my killer, my destroyer, my everything.

The day I moved to Washington DC May 1998. The defeated, solemn, sad expression on my face was just a reflection of the emptiness I lived on the inside. I felt like a walking corpse.

After moving to Washington I had a job within 6 weeks. I excelled on my job, developed and improved my technical and professional skills, and soon began making more money than I had ever made in SC. I appeared to "have it going on" to those around me. My family and those on the outside looking in began to look up to me, admire me even, but what they didn't know was that every night I contemplated when and where I was going to end it all. I found that the "old saying" *money can't buy happiness* to be true for me during this time. I had money, but no peace; I had money but no God.

I met some very good people, developed friendships, smiled all the time, yet living to die everyday.

Soon after learning my way around the city, I fell in love with Rock Creek Park. I decided that that would be THE PLACE that I would do it. I made many many visits to the park alone under the pretense that I was going there to read, but I was really there taking pills. I took pills many times there but always woke up hours later angry that I was still alive. I continued on this path for almost 4 years, but to no avail.

No one in my life in DC even had a clue that I was suicidal. I had become an expert at living a lie, and hiding my truth. I even became great at building walls and keeping others at bay.

After many failed attempts to end my life, I decided it was time to leave DC and move back to South Carolina to be near my parents.

May 1, 2003, I moved back home to Sumter, SC. In addition to being suicidal, I became afraid and uneasy about living in the nation's capital with all of the many terrorist attacks that were going on around us. I was even afraid for my girls attending school in the city.

I wanted out. So one weekend after visiting with my parents, I cried all the way back to DC and told my daughters it was time to go back home. They didn't want to move back but I knew that I had to try to save their lives even though I was trying to end mine. So against their wishes, I moved back to Sumter and back to my home church, Salem Missionary Baptist. I figured since I couldn't die, maybe, just maybe I'll get healed in church.

Now here it is May 2003 and I am back home in the church, working with the youth ministry (specifically the Praise Dance Ministry). I had money, my children, my parents, and many bonus children that God placed in my care. One would think that surely this woman is happy. NOT SO.

Even though most of my days, my time was spent surrounded by others, I went to bed miserable and crying every night. I still hated Angela. I still hated living. I still wanted to die.

No one told me that I had to renew my mind. No one told me that I had to walk in forgiveness. I lived my life holding on to every bad thing that had ever been done to me. My mind was poisoned and I didn't even have the strength or desire to ask God to Help Me. Was I alone yet? Had God forsaken me? I thought so.

I gave up on the idea of ever being happy. I didn't believe in love anymore. I had settled in my mind and heart that aside from the children in my life, no one would ever love me or want to be with me.

On October 20, 2004, while sitting in my car in the parking lot of Piggly Wiggly waiting for my mom to come out of the store, a little purple Corvette pulled up beside me. I looked over and this man with a gold tooth was smiling and winking at me. I said to my daughters, "If this little boy doesn't get out of my face I am going to curse him out." I didn't know it then, but that was the day I met the man who would become my husband. I rolled down my window and reluctantly took his phone number. The very first thing out of his mouth when I called him was, "You are my God-send". I thought to myself, what a joke this joker is. But…we started dating anyway.

His name was Shawn Foxworth, and a few weeks into the relationship I realized this man was NOT for me. He was from the streets, we had totally different backgrounds, upbringing, likes and dislikes. We had absolutely nothing in common. So why stay with him? Let my children tell it, I was sprung. Actually I thought I could change him. But what happened is I changed *me* to fit in with *him* in *his* world.

He was a heavy drinker so I started drinking daiquiris, wine coolers, and later wine and mixed drinks. He cursed like a sailor so I began cursing as much if not more than he did. He hung out and did everything he was big and bad enough to do so I did the same. I got lost in him. I made Shawn bigger than God.

Our relationship became a very toxic one to say the least. We fought regularly. I was abused and I was an abuser. I didn't care that my daughters or his children witnessed the bad behavior or heard the foul language. I didn't love me so why should he. I had come to expect the worse for me so it was easy to accept the worse. This destructive path continued for six years; six years of being with a man who brought out the worst in me. I was told by him that I was the worst woman he had ever been with, and he had been with many. I hated him as much as I loved him. Sounds crazy right? I know.

I was crazy. My life was crazy. My thoughts were crazy. Therefore, my actions were crazy.

February 2007, I had had enough. Of what? EVERYTHING. LIVING. HURTING. FIGHTING. NOT FIGHTING. LIVING. AND LIVING.

I recall waking up at 6:00am one Saturday morning to the voice of the enemy telling me to leave, it's time. SO I got out of my bed, grabbed my bag and tip-toed out of the bedroom and down the hall so that I wouldn't awaken Shawn or my daughters. I drove to Simpson Hardware and purchased a bag of Sulfur and a large container of rat poison. I then drove to the Rite Aid Drug Store where I purchased a large bottle of Tylenol PM, a large bottle of Excedrin PM, 1 box of sleeping pills, and 2 (20oz) ginger ale sodas. Then I went to the Travelers' Inn and got a room.

Once I got inside the room, I spread the letters out on my bed. The letters…yes those were the letters that I had written and carried around with me since 1995. I had a letter written to each of my 5 children, to my parents, one to my brother Porkey, one to my sister Rabbit, one to God, and I wrote one that day to Shawn. In these letters I asked for forgiveness if my death had hurt them. I pleaded with them to go on with their lives and to be better than I was. I even had the audacity to say, "I love you" to each of them.

I proceeded to mix up a concoction of the sulfur and rat poison with water as I was taking the pills that I had purchased. I drank the mixture of poison until I threw up, and every time I threw up I would mix up another glass until all of the containers were empty.

I laid down for 10 minutes, a very long 10 minutes and didn't die. So I got up, gathered my letters, and left. I drove back to the drug store and purchased two more boxes of sleeping pills. As I was taking these pills while driving, I remember thinking to myself that I would drive to Interstate 95 and by the time I got there I should pass out and a big truck would crash into me, killing me and no one would know that it was a suicide. That way my children could collect on the life insurance policy.

I didn't realize then that God had His hand on me. I never made it to I-95. As a matter of fact, I never made it off of Broad Street. I passed out a few minutes after leaving the drug store the second time. Somehow, my car ended up in the parking lot of the Gamecock Bowling Lane on Broad Street. I was told that a lady who was leaving passed by my car, saw me slumped over the steering wheel, and went inside and got help. The Help? A man who was bowling with his family and who "just happened" to be a doctor. I was told that he recognized that I had overdosed and called 911.

The story doesn't end there…I died. Yes my heart stopped in the ambulance enroute to the hospital and that same man, who rode to the hospital in the ambulance with me, revived me. (I know now that that moment in time was my BUT GOD moment).

I awoke in the hospital to my brother, Min. James Goodman standing on my left side, my sister, Min. Mary Ragins standing on my right side, and each of my children standing around the room looking at me crying. I went right back out after seeing their faces, but not before hearing my brother and my sister praying and saying, "Devil you can't have her."

I would love to tell you that after that ordeal I finally got it right and never attempted suicide again, but that would not be the truth. I continued on the destructive path for yet a few more years..

My relationship with Shawn became even more toxic after that experience. He couldn't understand or accept how or why I wanted to hurt myself, so our arguments and fights became more and more frequent and I was the crazy woman.

Six years of leaving Shawn only to go right back to him; fighting him, fighting with other women, calling his job, calling the police on him and having the police called on me; and still we remained together (if you can call that together). June 1, 2009 I moved out and actually stayed gone for six months. December 2009 we got back together, after promising each other to make changes and to get married.

I remember calling my brother, Min. James Goodman, (who was not my pastor yet) to tell him about my plans to marry Shawn. I called him because I wanted him to tell me not to do it. But to my surprise when I told him I was going back to Shawn and we were getting married and we wanted him to marry us, he said, "I would be honored". So I asked him, "Don't you want to pray about this thing first? I am your sister." His exact words to me were, "God has already shown me that he is the man for you". I couldn't see it but I trusted my brother and believed that God was with him. So we were married in a small ceremony on March 20, 2010.

Now don't think that all was well. During the tumultuous relationship and marriage with Shawn I attempted suicide more times than a few. I woke up in Tuomey Hospital so many times that only God kept them from putting me in an institution. I was so unstable that I was taking pills every time I was left alone.

Our first year of marriage was as bad as the crazy relationship leading up to the marriage. As a matter of fact, I didn't even change my last name to Foxworth for the entire first year of our marriage. I said, "It's not going to last anyway so why bother. I'll keep the name my daddy gave me so I won't have to change it back later." (You see I entered my marriage with a messed up mindset, therefore, I was living in my marriage with that same messed up mindset). I didn't know then that CHANGE was NECESSARY.

One day in May of 2010, my brother called me and told me that he has to do what God called him to do and it was time, he was starting his ministry. I said to him, "When and where?" My husband and I were not in any church and our marriage was going nowhere. We needed help. I needed help. I felt that this was it. So on May 10, 2010, Pastor James Goodman started A.L.I.V.E Praise & Worship Center & Ministries. We were two of the first six that sat with him in the beginning. I soon realized that my brother was not just my brother, but a Man of God that was sent to help me.

I remember calling him one day shortly after A.L.I.V.E's weekly Bible Study at the hotel and I said to him, "I hope you mean what you are doing because this is my last chance. I won't make it if you fail. I can't go anywhere else." He said to me, "I am real. I know I have y'all souls in my hand. This is it". For weeks, even months after that phone conversation I listened to God's Word being taught by Pastor G. I took notes. I understood. Then I went home and my husband and I continued to fight. We kept going to church and kept going home and fighting. Pastor Goodman would come over and counsel while First Lady Goodman would be on the phone praying. And in the midst of all of this, I was still attempting suicide regularly. **But one night…**

One Thursday night (around May 2011) while in Bible Study, Pastor Goodman said to the congregation, "A year from now none of y'all will be the same." I looked around at everyone in the room that night and wrote in my notes, "God that is for everyone except me." Oh how happy I am now that I was wrong. I thought that way because my home life was still in turmoil, my marriage was a mess, and we were still fighting after almost every service. It seemed like *"church"* wasn't doing us any good. And *"church"* wasn't doing us any good. However, Pastor and First Lady kept helping, kept praying, kept counseling us, and most importantly kept telling us not to stop, just keep coming to church. So we kept fighting and kept going to church. Then one night it happened.

My husband and I got into an argument before leaving home for Bible Study. We argued and cursed all the way to church, even while in the church's parking lot. We got out of the truck, put on our 'church faces' and walked into the church together as if nothing was happening. Once inside, our Praise & Worship Team began singing, "I Give Myself Away So You Can Use Me." It was during the ministering of that song and my finally hearing the words of the song that I realized I needed to "give myself away" so that God could get some use out of me.

I found myself forgetting about myself, my husband, my marriage, even my daughters and focusing only on God. And at that moment I left my seat, laid on the altar and cried out to God. I surrendered ALL of me to Him. Needless to say, Pastor Goodman never taught Bible Study that night, but God definitely was in the place and changed my life **that night.** When I arose and took my seat I WAS CHANGED. I WAS DELIVERED. I WAS SET FREE.

God's Word began to take root in my life. After I surrendered all of me to Him, I stopped trying to change my husband and began working on myself daily. Once I allowed God's Word to work in my life, every aspect of my life got better. I became so focused on me and becoming a Doer of the Word of God, that I hadn't even noticed that my husband was changing too.

I got delivered and set free from every single yoke of bondage that Satan had on me. My husband stopped drinking. We stopped fighting. We began to allow God to reign in our home. We became a married couple. We started living our lives as people of God.

Shawn became MY Man of God and I had become HIS Woman of God.

In 2012, one year after Pastor Goodman declared that all of us would be different, I WAS different. My life was different. I, no we began living a life, having a marriage where God is the Head and we were His.

NOW, We are Happy. We are Effective. We are One. We are Fulfilled. We are a Help and an Example to those around us. I thank God for joining my husband and I together.
For what God has joined together, we will not let anyone or anything put asunder.

I can truly say that now I am ALIVE
I am an Active Witness
I am a Living Epistle
I am an Interceding Believer
I am a Victorious Christian
I am an Excited Example

My Testimony:

I first attempted suicide in 1995 in my bathroom while my children were small and asleep in the room across the hall. I didn't know it then that the first time I tried to take my life would become my journey of despair for over 17 years. In spite of the fact that I had been blessed with 5 beautiful, smart children and had been married to their father since graduating from high school, I suffered from manic depression, low self-esteem, and self-hatred. So my journey began...

After failing at committing suicide the first time, the second time, the fifth time, the tenth time, and countless times after that, I devised a plan that I thought would surely render me the results that I longed for...(death). I began collecting pills: sleeping pills, over-the-counter pain pills of various brands, and even other people's pills when I would go to their homes. **BUT GOD**... *Every Single Time* I attempted suicide, someone found me. I woke up in the hospital more times than I can count. I attempted suicide so many times that I tore the lining of my stomach so much so that I could not take any medication at all, not even what was prescribed to me by my doctor.

As the years passed on, I became more and more and more and more depressed and suicidal. To look upon me and see the smiles, hear the laughter, and engaging in in-depth conversations with me, one would have never known just how messed up I was; or that every day that I lived all I thought about was dying, and how soon I could do it. This became my lifestyle and it started in 1995 and continued until I died in 2007 and beyond.

Yes, I died…February 2007, I woke up at 6:00am. The enemy said this is the day and I said ok. I got up, got dressed, quietly grabbed my shoes and purse, walked down the hall in my house, got in my car, and checked out. No, nothing happened to trigger it. My daughters were asleep in their bedrooms and my boyfriend (now husband) was asleep in our bed. I didn't wake anyone, I just left. I went to Simpson Hardware and purchased a bag of Sulfur and a bottle of rat poison. I than proceeded to Eckerd's Drug Store and purchased two large bottles of pain pills (Excedrin PM and Tylenol PM), and a pack of sleeping pills. I then went to the Travelers' Inn and got a room. I took the pre-written letters form my purse (one for each of my children, one for my parents, one for Shawn, one for my oldest sister Rabbit, and one for my oldest brother, who is now my Pastor). I laid the letters on the bed. I than began mixing up concoctions of all of the items I had just purchased and drank them. Every time I threw up I would make more and drink and I repeated this cycle until all of the containers were empty. I than took all of the pills and laid down. After about 10 minutes I realized that I was not dead, so I gathered up my letters and decided to go get more sleeping pills, drive to I-95 and by the time I get there a truck would crash into me and it will look like an accident. So I drove to the drug store and picked up 2 more packs of sleeping pills and began taking them while driving. **BUT GOD…** I never made it to I-95. Somehow, I ended up in the parking lot of the bowling alley, which was only about 1-2 miles from the drug store. After that I was out. I awoke in the hospital with my children, my brother James, and my sister, Mary Jane standing over me praying.

I was told that a man found me slumped over in my car, and he was a doctor and quickly recognized that I had overdosed. He rode with me in the ambulance. The doctor in the hospital later told me that I died en route to the hospital, but God brought me back. He also told me that my body absorbed most of the poisons that I had ingested.

No, I didn't stop trying even after that. I continued to attempt suicide time after time until 2011. That's when Pastor James Goodman walked into the hospital room where I laid after having my stomach pumped for the several hundredths time looked at me, pointed his finger at me, and said, "This is the last time you will be here. Now get ahold of God's Word and live." He then walked out, taking my husband with him. (of course, by this time I was married to my husband Shawn, and had joined and started attending ALIVE Praise & Worship Center & Ministries)…this is where Pastor Goodman was teaching God's Word with clarity, simplicity, and understanding. But with all the Word I was being taught I was still in bondage in my mind. It wasn't until 2012 (the year of my deliverance) when I went to Bible Study one Thursday night and decided that I had had enough. *I WAS SICK AND TIRED OF BEING SICK AND TIRED.* And that time I laid on the alter, cried out to God, and surrendered all of me to Him. I gave Him all of me, my children, my husband, my life. From that day until this present time, I have been walking in my Total and Complete Deliverance.

I am Angela Goodman-Foxworth, a Woman of God, and I AM FREE. I AM DELIVERED. I AM WHOLE. I AM CALLED BY GOD TO HELP OTHERS GET DELIVERED AND SET FREE.

www.ingramcontent.com/pod-product-compliance
Lightning Source LLC
Chambersburg PA
CBHW031618040426
42452CB00006B/576